MW01273377

Who Killed Spalding Gray?

Also by Daniel MacIvor

who killed Spalding Gray?
Daniel MacIvor

Playwrights Canada Press
Toronto

For professional or amateur production rights, please contact:
The Gary Goddard Agency
149 Church Street, 2nd Floor Toronto, ON M5B 1Y4
416-928-0299, meaghan@garygoddardagency.com

LIBRARY AND ARCHIVES CANADA CATALOGUING IN PUBLICATION
MacIvor, Daniel, 1962-, author
    Who killed Spalding Gray? / Daniel MacIvor. -- First edition.

A play.
Issued in print and electronic formats.
ISBN 978-1-77091-834-4 (softcover).--ISBN 978-1-77091-835-1 (PDF).--
ISBN 978-1-77091-836-8 (EPUB).--ISBN 978-1-77091-837-5 (Kindle)

    1. Gray, Spalding, 1941-2004--Drama. 2. MacIvor, Daniel, 1962-
--Drama. I. Title.

PS8575.I86W56 2017   C812'.54   C2017-906257-3
                                                     C2017-906258-1

We acknowledge the financial support of the Canada Council for the Arts, the Ontario Arts Council (OAC), the Ontario Media Development Corporation, and the Government of Canada for our publishing activities.

Once again, and finally,
for Iris

Who Killed Spalding Gray? was developed by reWork Productions with the support of Necessary Angel and Factory Theatre and presented by reWork and Canadian Stage at the Berkeley Street Downstairs Theatre, Toronto, from November 30 through December 11, 2016, with the following cast and creative team:

Performer: Daniel MacIvor

Director: Daniel Brooks
Producer for reWork: Marcie Januska
Dramaturge: Iris Turcott
Stage Manager: Marcie Januska
Lighting Designer: Kimberly Purtell

A table and a chair centre stage.

On stage left, a chair and a microphone.

On the table a microphone, a notebook and a glass of water.

Up centre a surface upon which projections may appear.

DANIEL *emerges with a second glass of water and the book* The Journals of Spalding Gray. *He puts the glass and book down on the table and sets up the two chairs and microphones in front of the table, side by side, as if for a seated interview.*

He goes into the audience and invites an audience member to the stage.

He seats them in one of the chairs and takes the other chair.

He asks the audience member to answer three questions. They may speak a bit broadly around these topics—other questions may ensue from the main questions (i.e., Where are you from? What do you do? Why did you come here?).

DANIEL

Who are you?

Who am I?

> *During this section DANIEL talks about the women in his life, those he has lost. He asks the audience member if they would share with him the name of a woman that they may have lost, someone they loved. Someone they still think of. If the audience member says they have not lost a woman of importance DANIEL asks simply for a name of a beloved woman in their life. Finally DANIEL asks:*

Who is Spalding Gray?

> *DANIEL helps the audience member back to their seat.*

> *He nods to the booth to start sound.*

> *We hear a section of an audio session with ELLAE, a Psychic Intuitive in Oregon.*

> *DANIEL replaces the chairs and microphones. He places the second glass of water beside the second chair.*

ELLAE

The thing about seeing Spalding Gray in St. Louis was this spectre of depression. But you're going to do the opposite thing here. The tricky part

is you don't want to welcome him in a way that he gets m
with this side of the school of life, so that in any way that his passage
has not been completed you make it more difficult for him to leave. So,
history is made up of people, people either taking responsibility for what
they've done or being memorialized by others and it's like footprints that
they leave behind, and it's called their legacy or their memory or their
gift and it empowers them to move forward in their journey, to know
that they have left something here. So very simply a welcome would be
"onward with the journey" and he will respond according to who he
is—you can't guarantee anything—but you would be giving him the
tools for completion."

> *DANIEL goes to the table and sits.*

> *He stares at the audience.*

> *DANIEL looks at the glass of water.*

> *Slide: "The Ocean."*

> *DANIEL drinks the whole glass of water down.*

> *Light shift.*

DANIEL
I'm going to tell you the truth.

I am not Spalding Gray, as we've established, I am Daniel MacIvor.

And once upon a time I had a theatre company that I ran with my business partner. We were a touring theatre company based in Toronto and we travelled all over the word. And sometimes we'd get letters. Mostly these letters were telling us how much they liked the work. People who didn't like the work didn't bother to write letters. People who didn't like the work didn't have to write letters because people who didn't like the work usually worked for the newspaper. Ha.

One day we got a letter. It was addressed to me but my business partner opened it; she always opened the mail. It was a letter from a guy. I asked my business partner to show it to me but she wouldn't. I asked her, "Is it romantic?" and she said, "No, it's creepy."

Also during this time I was making movies. And in 2003 I went to Nova Scotia to direct a movie I had written. While I was making this movie I met a guy and we started dating.

On our first date the guy tells me that he had once written me a letter and I had never responded. I asked him what he said in the letter. And he told me a story about how years ago he had been in a bookstore and he found himself inexplicably drawn to a section of the bookstore he never visited before, and then he was inexplicably drawn to a particular book. And he picked up the book and it was my book. Well it was a play but they're still

0t WHO KILLED SPALDING GRAY?

called books. He didn't know that it was my book but when he turned the book over and saw my picture his whole body started vibrating and he knew that one day we would be together. He had told that story in the letter he sent me. And some people might call that creepy but at the time I found it very romantic.

By the time I was back in Toronto editing the movie we had split up. For those of you who know about filmmaking that means it lasted about four months. And it was a somewhat acrimonious breakup. That has been my romantic pathology: short with a bad ending. One day while I was on a break from editing I saw that I had a call from the ex-boyfriend: "Call me." So on the next break I called him and he told me that he had been on the phone that morning with his Intuitive in Oregon—an Intuitive is basically what used to be called a psychic—they don't really like the name psychic with its implications of gypsies and crystal balls. And "Intuitive" looks better on a business card. So the ex-boyfriend told me that on the phone his Intuitive had asked him if he had someone in his life named Daniel. He said yes in fact he did. And she told him that this Daniel was in great danger. She said this Daniel had an entity attached to him and it was trying to kill him and he had to have it removed. Now at the time I didn't really care about danger or entities or whatever; I was more suspicious of the ex-boyfriend's motives. So I got a bit cocky said, "Well if she has something to say to me she can tell me herself, give me her number." And so he called my bluff and gave me her number.

7

So on the lunch break I thought, "What the hell," and I give her a call. And we talk for a long long time. And she tells me a lot of things. Not things like the past or the future but things about feelings. She described feelings that were very familiar to me. Feelings of never fitting in, feelings of always being outside life, feelings of a chronic dis-ease. And I suppose many people would identify with those feelings, perhaps many people here, but it wasn't so much what she said, it was more how she said it, there was a . . . something else. And I wept.

In fact I still talk to her now; her name is Ellae Elinwood, that was her voice you heard earlier. She lives in Wyoming now. I even talked to her about what was going to happen here with this ritual tonight. But back then, the first day I talked to her, she told me these feelings I was having were due to the entity and I would have to have the entity removed. But she couldn't remove it. But she knew someone who could. His name was Paul Goodberg. And he was in San Rafael, California. And so I made arrangements to go.

Go.

Music starts. It is a vocal-free version of "This Must Be the Place" by the Talking Heads.

I would always put this song on when I wanted to dance, but the song always made me so sad I never danced.

DANIEL sings a couple of verses of the song.

The music stops abruptly and blackout.

In the black he gets up from the table.

I need to tell you a story.

Light.

His name, the man in the story, is Howard.

For reasons we don't need to get into, Howard has always wanted to kill himself.

So Howard decides its time and thinks at some length about killing himself. Not about if he will or if he won't, he's been through all that already. His whole life the question has never been "if" it's been "how."

So. Hanging? Well for hanging one would need a great height, the quick death of the broken neck, otherwise it's strangulation, which is unappealing in that a hanging death by strangulation could take three minutes or more of kicking and regret. Poison? Well poison's not entirely dependable. And most often in cases of poisoning one dies as the result of choking on their own vomit. And that would be a bit of a mess for some poor soul to have to clean up. Jumping? Howard's never been a fan of heights. A gun? Well that would be loud. And messy. The slitting of wrists? Perhaps in a bathtub? Tidy indeed that way. But would it hurt? Would he have the courage to draw blade on tender skin? Howard thinks not. Of course there's always carbon monoxide, the car running in the garage. But that's been done to death. Drowning? Drowning. Perhaps drowning.

He has an odd moment with the empty glass of water on the desk behind him.

No no no no no . . . No not for the story of Howard.

In this story the man, Howard, decides that no decision would be best. Howard decides it would be best if it happened not *by* him but *to* him. To be blindsided.

And so Howard talks to a man who sends him to a woman who gives him the number of a man who arranges a meeting in a motel room with Don. Don. Dawn. Dusk. Dawn. Dusk and Dawn. Don Horchuk. Don Horchuk is a contractor of sorts. A man who can fix things.

Howard, meet Don; Don, meet Howard.

Light shift.

HOWARD

I don't want it to hurt.

DON

You don't want it to hurt?

HOWARD

I don't want anything like that.

DON

You don't want anything like that.

HOWARD

No.

DON

You just want to die.

HOWARD

Yes.

DON

So kill yourself.

HOWARD

I can't.

DON
Why not?

HOWARD
Because . . .

DON
Religious?

HOWARD
No.

DON
So why?

HOWARD
I'm afraid.

DON
Of what?

HOWARD
That I'll fail.

DON
And you don't want to fail.

HOWARD

No.

DON

You depressed? They got pills for that, you know.

HOWARD

I don't want any more pills.

DON

You want to die.

HOWARD

Yes.

DON

Why?

HOWARD

I don't fit.

DON

You don't fit.

HOWARD

Nothing fits.

DON

Nothing fits.

HOWARD

No.

DON

Well, nothing fits like it used to.

HOWARD

It never did. I just pretended.

DON

Who's not pretending?

HOWARD

Are you?

DON

Well there you go my friend. Harold is it?

HOWARD

Howard.

DON

Howard?

HOWARD

Howard.

DON

How. Well there you go How. No I am not pretending. This is the real shit right here, How. Walk the walk, talk the talk. Feelings, fuck feelings. Doing. That's the thing.

HOWARD

Yes.

DON

So do it.

HOWARD

I want you to do it for me.

DON

You got a family?

HOWARD

Not anymore.

DON

They dead?

HOWARD
Might as well be.

DON
Kids.

HOWARD
No.

After a moment.

A son.

DON
Ah, kids.

HOWARD
Yeah.

DON
Wife left?

HOWARD
She was never there.

DON
Ah, you're a poet aren't you How.

HOWARD

No.

DON

Anyway, so what? There's lots of fish in the sea.

HOWARD

I've been thinking about drowning but I don't want to be eaten.

DON

It's not like you'd feel it.

HOWARD

I guess.

DON

So no drowning?

HOWARD

Could you do that?

DON

Follow you along the coast one night. Good nudge of the bumper into the bay. Can't open those doors underwater.

HOWARD

Maybe not.

DON

But maybe?

HOWARD

I don't want to know.

DON

Oh you won't.

HOWARD

So you'll do it?

DON

Somebody's got to do it.

HOWARD

Shake?

DON

Sure.

Light shift.

DANIEL

The two men shake hands. Howard feels relieved. Even Don feels relieved for Howard—you don't have to know Howard's story to feel his sadness. Howard leaves the motel room and goes home and imagines that soon all this will be over. Don leaves the motel room and goes home and during the night has a massive coronary and dies in his bed alone.

DANIEL goes to the table and sits.

Spalding Gray has been described by people as a brilliant, charismatic man.

Spalding Gray told stories. He said that they were true. But I'm not entirely sure that they were.

The first true story he told was in 1977, it was called *Rumstick Road* and it told the story of his mother's suicide by carbon-monoxide poisoning in the family garage at the age of fifty-two in 1967.

That went well, so he told many more true stories.

There were some stories that he didn't tell.

And there was one story he couldn't tell.

The story he couldn't tell took place on January 10, 2004, in New York City and in it he takes his son to see Tim Burton's movie *Big Fish* and after the movie Spalding Gray sits in the theatre and he weeps. And then he takes his son to their SoHo loft and leaves him there with his stepdaughter. He tells them he's going to a meeting but he doesn't go to a meeting. Instead he rides the Staten Island Ferry back and forth and back and forth and back and forth for the rest of his life.

I tell stories and I say they are not true, but I'm not sure that they're not.

Some people say that I'm afraid of you but I want you to like me.

I could never understand how that could be true, but now I see that those are both the same thing.

Light shift.

It's January 10, 2004, and I've flown across the country to see Paul Goodberg who specializes in entities. Paul Goodberg lives in San Rafael, California, and the entity apparently lives in me.

I'm no expert on entities but I have been in contact with those who are and they would tell you than an entity is basically energy that's released from the body at death. Now any death releases energy from the body but in particular kinds of deaths—murders, accidents, suicides—especially suicides—an entity can be formed. This is because these deaths—murders, accidents, suicides—break the contract. The experts would say that life is a contract with time and the contract must be seen out, so in these "breaking the contract" deaths the energy gets stuck between life and death and an entity is formed. Now some entities are benign and they just hang around waiting for the contract to run out and then they pass on, but some entities are malevolent and they try to attach themselves to a living body so they can rejoin life. Basically they want your body and are trying to kill you. Sitting on your shoulder, whispering in your ear, needing you alive but wanting you dead. It's fucked up.

Experts in entities can see them anywhere. Those who know about such things would say this room is filled with entities. Apparently those who have had an entity can especially see them. They might say there is an entity sitting in that chair over there. But I'm no expert on entities.

I'm also no expert on San Rafael but I can tell you it's about thirty minutes from San Francisco across the Golden Gate Bridge on the San Rafael Bay and it's really "San Ra-fi-el" but the locals call it "San Ra-fell." I had flown into San Francisco the night before and driven to San Rafael and taken a room at a B & B where I was to say that night and the next and perhaps a third depending on how The Work went—that's what Paul Goodberg called it: "The Work." It's probably significant enough to mention that I hadn't had a drink in a couple of months, ever since I talked to Ellae because she had suggested I was drinking so much because I was medicating the entity—not in fact because I was an alcoholic, well that's a relief, I'll have to tell my entire family of alcoholics—and also she said it was best I not drink so I would be clear in preparation for The Work. As a result of not drinking I found it hard to fall asleep at night and harder to wake up in the morning. This particular morning at the B & B though I had no problem waking up because in the lot next door the neighbours were in the middle of a full-on build from scratch of a house. A House. This I found very significant because the book of mine that the ex-boyfriend had picked up in the bookstore was called *House*. I look for significance where I can find it.

So I'm in the office of Paul Goodberg but I'm not sure what I'm supposed to be doing. Fortunately Paul Goodberg tells me that I don't have to do anything at all.

So I look around the office. It could have been a therapist's office. Off-white walls, beige leather couch and matching armchair, nondescript modern art, a couple of ferns, a bookcase taking up one wall. And this was where things got different, on the bookcase was every sort of religious icon you could imagine: Celtic cross, African fertility symbol, crystals, Hindu gods, Christian saints, a menorah, a Buddha. I thought, well that's probably very comforting to people who believe in things because they would see their particular belief represented. It was even comforting to me who believed in none of them, or probably more truly: all of them.

But Paul Goodberg is not a therapist. He is a Psychic Surgeon. Now there are two kinds of Psychic Surgeons. One type of

Psychic Surgeon exists in hot little storefronts in Latin American countries and the Philippines, where brown men in cream suits tend to long lines of well-heeled white people by non-surgically removing their tumours and growths. Tumours and growths that suspiciously resemble grapes dipped in cow's blood and chicken livers. They are the impossiblists with their emotional placebos. But Paul Goodberg is not that type of Psychic Surgeon. He doesn't deal with tumours and growths. At least not of the physical kind.

Light shift.

We hear another section of a session with ELLAE, *the Oregon Intuitive.*

DANIEL *rises and replaces the first glass of water with the second.*

ELLAE

Actually most of the old religions have amazing ceremonies for people who have committed suicide—they're ceremonies that really help: turn toward the light, extinguish all need to be here, take responsibility for your personal journey. And it isn't just suicide, Daniel, it's violent death, it's car accidents, it could be someone killed by another person; there's no fairness in it, it's just when timing is violated period. You'd be particularly good at this because you've had one of those guys inside of you. I mean you know the communion that entities can form with a human being and the relationship that can happen and how destructive

*it is. I know of someone who got rid of his entity and missed it so much
he went ahead and killed himself anyway. It is a very treacherous realm.*

From the darkness:

DANIEL
On the first day . . .

Light.

. . . after meeting Don in the motel room on the highway,
Howard wakes up and he drives to the ocean. A brilliant, charismatic man once said that the ocean was one of the only four real
things in life? The ocean, the sky, swimming and . . . One more.

In any event, Howard drove to the ocean the morning after his
meeting with Don Horchuk, the man who could fix things.
For Howard the ocean trip was a kind of respite, a safe haven
for a moment or two. Trips to the ocean weren't common for
Howard so unless he'd been followed it wasn't likely that he
would be blindsided at the ocean. More likely it would happen
outside his condo, or in front of the deli he ate at daily or in the
parking lot of the gym he oddly had every intention of continu-
ing to renew his monthly membership with. Not here in this
new place, the ocean. Not a new place in Howard's thinking
though; the ocean took up much of Howard's thinking since his
recent fear of downing.

And in the dream I . . .

> *DANIEL has an odd moment with the glass of water on the table behind him.*

Not yet.

And Howard sat on a bench, a bench some thoughtful city councillor had famously fought to have placed here in this spot near the few remaining trees at the shore, sheltered yet with a clear view of the ocean.

The ocean the ocean. Yearning for the moon yet confined by the earth. The infinite uncertain.

And Howard felt a pain in his heart. His broken heart. And he thought briefly of his ex-wife. That saint.

Then he thought of his son. A story about a kite. A painful story.

Would his son care when he was gone? He wouldn't. Would he? He wouldn't he wouldn't he wouldn't he wouldn't he wouldn't he wouldn't he wouldn't. He wouldn't.

Then Howard thought about Don.

Howard wondered if he'd been followed.

The ocean. What a terrible place to die.

And Howard felt afraid.

Of course he needn't have though, because Don Horchuk the man who could fix things could not fix, as it turned out, his very own heart. Now cold and dead in his bed.

On his way back to the table, DANIEL takes a sudden U-turn and dashes toward the mic.

Light shift.

HELENA BONHAM CARTER
Hello, I'm Helena Bonham Carter and I'd like to tell you two stories. The first story is the story of a film I was in. A beautiful film directed by my ex, the American film director Tim Burton. That film is called *Big Fish*.

I haven't seen the film in a while, but I played two parts so I remember it very well. In fact I'll be playing two parts tonight, lucky me. I'll be playing myself, Helena Bonham Carter, and later I'll also be playing the mysterious young woman with the name tag that Howard meets at a sushi stall.

Some people say that *Big Fish* is Tim's best film. If I believed that to be true it would be ill-advised of me on many fronts to say so.

Big Fish is a story of a man played in later life by Albert Finney and as a younger man by Ewan McGregor who tells elaborate tales that some people believe are true and some people, mostly his son—played by Billy Crudup—think are lies. But in the end the point of the film is that the stories all turn out to be true. Although Tim would disagree; he'd say the point is it doesn't matter if the stories are true or not. But I like to think they're true. I suppose Tim and I would agree that the point truly is that in the end the son realizes there is no such thing as a lie if you're a storyteller.

The second story is the story of how *Big Fish* is the last film that Spalding Gray saw. He saw it on the last day of his life. And when the film was over Spalding Gray sat in the theatre and wept.

People have said that *Big Fish* is sunny. Sunnier for Tim at least. I don't think I would call it sunny. I think I would say that it is heartbreaking. And at the centre of that broken heart lives regret. Crushing regret.

Mostly people loved the film. Of course some people hated it as people will. Roger Ebert in the *Chicago Sun-Times* said something like . . . Oh I don't remember really . . . "Burton has been recycling the same skills over and over again and desperately requires someone to walk in and demand that he get to the point. This is doodling of a very high order." Or something . . . But at the end of the day in terms of what people say about Tim or his work he doesn't give a creeping fuck. Nor do I—although I have suffered a "*critical* depression" or two in my time. As apparently was the case with Spalding Gray.

DANIEL returns to the table.

He reads:

DANIEL
Nineteen eighty-seven. Pauline Kael writing in *The New Yorker* on *Swimming to Cambodia*, written and performed by Spalding Gray.

"Spalding Gray is an actor who has discovered strong material and he builds the tension—his words come faster, his voice gets louder. He thinks like an actor; he doesn't know that heating up his piddling stage act by an account of the Cambodian misery is about the most squalid thing anyone could do."

Two thousand and six. Robert Cushman writing in *The National Post* on *Here Lies Henry* written and performed by Daniel MacIvor.

"It seems futile to ponder whether or not a fictitious character is telling the truth. I know this may well be the point—the unreliable narrator and all that—but it's never struck me as a very interesting one. Which raises the question, one that arises in nearly every MacIvor play that I've seen: Who cares?"

Now I'm not comparing myself to Spalding Gray as an artist—
although some will accuse me of that—but I'm not. I'm just
saying I understand what it's like to have your feelings hurt.

Light shift.

So it's January 10, 2004, in San Rafael, California. I'm in the
office of Paul Goodberg, Psychic Surgeon, and I'm lying on the
couch as instructed. Paul Goodbeg tells me that I can do whatever I want: I can read a book; I can fall asleep; he'll just go into
his trance and then let me know when he's back. But I didn't
bring a book and I can't sleep. Paul Goodberg seems to have
no trouble sleeping though because about two minutes after he
goes into his trance he's snoring. Or perhaps people in trances
snore? I don't know, I'm no expert on trances.

So I lie there feeling like a fool. What am I doing here? But
my life has more and more been spinning out of control. It got
to the point where I had to sell my house in Toronto because
all the crack dealers knew where I lived. We'd become such
good friends that when they didn't see me around for a while
they'd pop by to check on me because they were worried about
me, and when it gets to the point where your crack dealer is
concerned about your well-being it's time to move to Halifax.
And I quickly rented an apartment without investigating the

neighbourhood too much and lo and behold it's smack dab in the middle of the crack neighbourhood. So well what's a guy to do when he's just moved in? A guy's going to want to get to know his neighbours! So one night while I'm hanging out with some of my new neighbours I decide it's probably a good idea to give one of my new friends my bank card and PIN to go out and get some more money for more crack because I don't want to go because why? Well, it's chilly out. Really? So considering all that it's better that I'm here in San Rafael on the couch. And no matter what, no matter what happens, just showing up here and going through whatever this might be, is a choice toward life and away from . . . the other. So I make peace with that.

Six hours pass. Finally Paul Goodberg comes out of his trance—or wakes up. And he tells me that he has made contact with the entity and I am to come back tomorrow and he's going to ask it to leave. Why the hell didn't he just ask it to leave when he met it? And as I'm heading out he says, "I hope I won't have to kill it." The plot thickens.

So I go back to the B & B and I'm not sure what I did. Probably read some Jack Kornfield or Pema Chödrön. I was in a delicate state. I do remember that I found a matchbook sitting on the desk. It was black with a white illustration and advertising something or other—a restaurant I think—and I opened it up and it had an inscription inside which I found significant. I found the inscription so significant that I put the matchbook in my papers, somewhere special, so I'd save it forever. So special a place in fact that I have never found it since. I don't remember exactly what the inscription said. Of course I do but I don't want to tell you. It's embarrassing. It said "Find Romance." And I find that embarrassing because I found it so significant. I'm embarrassed to be telling you this right now. And I find it more embarrassing than the fact that I just told you I used to smoke crack. Why am I so embarrassed about that? Well because my fear is that some day I'll die and—that's not my fear, dying—my fear is that some day I'll be dead and some grad student will be going through my papers in my archive and find the matchbook and open it and see "Find Romance" and think how significant that was to me and say: "Oh so that's all he ever really wanted." And I'm not sure why exactly that's so embarrassing because maybe that is all I ever really wanted. And why is that so embarrassing that maybe that's all I ever wanted? Because I'm so fucking bad at it. Terrible at it. A master of misery. I'm like a guy who really really wants to play the piano but doesn't have any fingers. When it comes to love I am fingerless. And it's not the fingerlessness that's so bad, it's the longing to play the piano. The longing for something I will never have. And that's sad. And your pity for my sadness? *That* is embarrassing.

Anyway, matchbook, matchbook, matchbook, and after that I'm not sure what I did. I probably looked out the window at the significant building lot next door and then imagined I was in a movie, the camera panning across the building lot and then moving around the B & B, through the trees behind and around the corner again, back into the lot, and then the camera pans and turns and sees me in the window. Closer, closer, closer, and now I'm in the dream.

And in the dream I look like this. And there's a mountain and a Ferris wheel and if I turn this way it's all water. Like the ocean. But more so. And warmer. And it's above me as well. And I'm floating in it. Like sky. I'm floating in it. But I don't know.

Blackout.

Slide: "The Sky."

In the dark:

On the first day . . .

Light.

. . . after Howard met Don at the motel on the highway and Howard went to the ocean and sat on the bench at the shore, Howard thought about a story about a kite.

Howard had a son. And one day Howard took his son out to fly a kite. It was the kind of story that might have a soundtrack. And the sky is clear and blue. There's a green hill just like there should be and Howard's son comes running down the hill with the kite they had bought that morning at the mall. "Not some cheap factory kite"—that's what Howard had said to the clerk at the store—"not some Chinese kite"—Howard said—"an American kite." And Howard's son keeps running down the hill with his American kite, but he can't seem to catch a wind. Over and over again. And each time the nose of the kite keeps hitting the hill, digging up tufts of earth and grass, making a tuck-tuck-tuck-tuck-tucking sound all the way down the hill. And Howard thinks, "What's wrong with that kid he can't catch a breeze." Over and over. Running down the hill. Tuck tuck tuck tuck. Tuck tuck tuck tuck tuck. And Howard gets angry. He gets so angry and he goes over and grabs his son by the jacket and he picks up the kite and he strides back to the car and he tosses his son in the front seat and he throws the kite in the trunk and he slams the trunk and gets in the car beside his son and he looks at his son and says: "You couldn't catch a breeze in a windstorm." And Howard and his son drive silently toward home, the kite in the trunk, never to be thought of again.

Until this day, here on the bench by the ocean, Howard remembering the kite and the blue sky and green hill and his son trying trying trying so hard Howard realizes, in a tiny moment, the kind of tiny moment that has walls and a floor and a ceiling and a small, perfect window, the kind of perfect window that frames everything in a way that you've never seen it before, and here looking through the perfect window of the tiny moment Howard realizes there was no breeze to catch that day; there was no wind.

Soundtrack music.

And Howard sees for the first time—here on the bench on the beach by the ocean the day after meeting Don Horchuk in the motel room on the highway—Howard sees through the perfect window of the tiny moment, that it was his own fault that he had picked a day with no wind.

"It was my fault."

"It was my fault."

And then something happens, here on the bench Howard sees that day again, but now through the perfect window of the tiny moment: Howard sees the day that might have been, where there was a breeze. And the kite lifts off, up and high, both he and his boy holding the string, feeling the pull of the air above. Like fishing in the sky. That's what it feels like, like fishing in the sky. And Howard feels like a tingle, like a pulse, like a surging in his broken heart. The sky clear and blue. The green hill. The perfect breeze. The American kite. Rising rising rising.

Music fades.

On the second day . . .

Light shift.

. . . after Howard met Don at the motel on the highway Howard's alarm goes off at eight but he stays in bed. He thinks about Don.

Most days Howard would lie in bed till nearly noon, watching the sun on the wall where it would come in the window and land where it did, and then move up the wall and across the ceiling and then off *to* wherever it would go next. Upstairs? Next door? But not today. Today there is no sun, so he just lies there.

Lunchtime. Howard gets up and gets dressed and leaves the condo. This is when he would normally feel it. The noonday demon. Sitting on his back. Whispering into his ear. Needing him alive but wanting him dead. But today it's quiet.

Howard walks through an open market. Fruits and nuts and strange smells. He's standing in front of a sushi stall. There's a young woman working there. She's wearing a name tag. Howard thinks about Don.

Howard considers sushi. He thinks about drowning. He should probably avoid fish, he thinks; he doesn't want to make them angry. Or maybe he should. Eat them before they eat him. Howard laughs.

HOWARD *laughs.*

The young woman looks at him. He reads her name tag.

Here DANIEL uses the name of the beloved woman that the audience member gave him during the opening interview.

BELOVED. She's pretty, Howard thinks. Too late. Too fucking late, Howard thinks. BELOVED looks at him and smiles.

Howard thinks about a California roll.

BELOVED
You want a California roll?

HOWARD
I was thinking about a California roll.

BELOVED
I know.

HOWARD
I guess everybody thinks about a California roll.

BELOVED
Not the way you do.

HOWARD
Oh. How do I think about a California roll?

BELOVED

You want the dish without the fish.

HOWARD

A California roll has fish.

BELOVED

No. It has crab. That's shellfish. It's seafood but not fish.

HOWARD

Oh.

BELOVED

And also, you're a Cancer.

HOWARD

How did you know I was a Cancer?

BELOVED

I can tell by your fingernails.

HOWARD

By my . . . ?

BELOVED

No. I can tell by your voice. You have a very nice voice.

HOWARD
No I don't.

BELOVED
I'm BELOVED.

HOWARD
Yes, I can see by your name tag.

BELOVED
Hello.

HOWARD
I think I'll have the salmon.

BELOVED
Are you going to tell me your name . . .

HOWARD
Am I going to . . . ?

BELOVED
. . . Howard?

HOWARD
How do you know my name?

BELOVED

I can see by your name tag.

HOWARD

By my . . . ?

BELOVED

By your fingernails.

HOWARD

By my . . . ?

BELOVED

By your voice.

HOWARD

Who are you?

BELOVED

BELOVED.

HOWARD

Do I know you?

BELOVED

It's not too late.

HOWARD
What?

BELOVED
It's not too fucking late.

HOWARD
It's not too late for what?

BELOVED
Do you want to kiss me?

HOWARD
Do I want to—?

BELOVED
—kiss me?

HOWARD
I don't know. Do I?

Pause.

BELOVED
You already are.

Light shift.

We hear Dinah Washington singing "What a Difference a Day Makes."

DANIEL goes to the table and picks up the notebook. As he dances to the music he holds the notebook up over his head like a sign and displays one word written on each page:

"THIS." "IS." "ALL." "YOUR." "FAULT."

He rips the last page (" FAULT") out of the notebook and hands it to the earlier interviewee and with their permission takes them on stage and waltzes with them.

He takes them back to their seat.

DANIEL goes back to the table.

Light shift.

DANIEL

My father was haunted. You could tell by his eyes. By the way he held himself, held his hammer, held his liquor. One night there was sickness in the house. My father and I. A virus. Not a metaphor. A real virus. Something like a flu. Something in the stomach. And we lay on the coach—we called it a chester-field—my father and I. Me cradled in his arms. Spooning. Both of us sick. A crystalline memory moment. Both of us taking turns vomiting into the same bucket there on the floor. Both of us weakened into allowing comfort from the warmth of one another's body. Nothing but two humans holding one another wrapped in a virus. And it felt like safe. Safely. Safety.

Slide: "Swimming."

Light shift.

January 11, 2004. San Rafael, California, in the office of Paul Goodberg, Psychic Surgeon. The second day on the couch.

And Paul Goodberg goes to sleep, or into his trance, and I lie on the couch for a couple of hours. Nothing is happening, nothing is happening. And then all of a sudden I start to vibrate. My whole body is vibrating like I'm going to fall off the couch. And then it just stops.

About an hour later Paul Goodberg comes out of his trance, or wakes up. He asks me if anything happened. And I tell him yes, and I explain about the vibrating and I tell him how the very same thing had happened to me once before when I was eleven years old and I was home from school with a fever. I was lying on the couch, we called it a chesterfield, and I was home alone. My father had been ill but recovered and went out on a bender to celebrate and my mother was at work; I was alone. And I was looking up at the ceiling and all of a sudden I could see this translucent ball of energy floating just below the ceiling and then it was as if there was an invisible scoop taking smaller balls off the big ball and throwing them at me and hitting me in the chest and making my whole body vibrate so hard I thought I was going to fall off the chesterfield. It was a feeling I had in my bones, and especially in my teeth. And I explained all this to Paul Goodberg. And Paul Goodberg was very calm and he said, "Well yes of course. Of course. That's when the entity entered you."

Of course.

Of course.

Of course.

Then Paul Goodberg says that unfortunately he had to kill the entity. I didn't ask how. Or why that was unfortunate. The plan was I'd come back tomorrow so he could make sure it was dead.

So I leave the office and I really want to feel different. I look everywhere for a sign. I walk by a bar. It's called The Broken Drum. Is that a sign? Well of course, it's a literal sign. What does a broken drum sound like? I go inside to find out. And while I'm there I think I'll just have a glass of wine. A nice glass of wine. Nothing wrong with a nice glass of wine. Nice people drink glasses of wine. Monks might have a nice glass of wine.

Mother Teresa probably liked a nice glass of wine. Though the jury's out how nice she was. Five glasses of wine and a couple of Jägers later I'm looking everywhere for a sign. I have an orange notebook and I'm writing down everything I hear, eavesdropping on conversations all around me: "My sex life is like the Sahara Desert"; "Tulsa has the best beer nights"; something I can't make out. Show me a sign! And then I notice that a TV is on in the corner in the room, hanging from the ceiling, and it's on CNN, and there's a news loop happening. One of those stories they repeat again and again with a kind of ferocity they save for natural disasters or dead celebrities. And I move closer to the TV to see what it is and I see the face of Spalding Gray. He's gone missing. They're telling the story of his day: he went to see the Tim Burton movie *Big Fish* with his son; he left his son at their SoHo loft; he was last seen on the Staten Island Ferry. And it wasn't good. You could tell it wasn't good. Was this my sign? And then I remembered something that Ellae told me, that sometimes two people can share an entity, and I have this overwhelming feeling that Spalding Gray going missing is somehow connected to my entity being removed. But no no no, why would I share an entity with Spalding Gray? What did we really have in common? Other than the obvious. I mean, what did I even feel about Spalding Gray really? Probably, honestly, jealousy. He was successful and famous and friends with all the cool kids, David Byrne, Laurie Anderson, Jonathan Demme. And what did he do that I didn't do? Sit at a table? Drink a glass of water?

He indicates the table and water before him.

So hey, now give *me* a fucking Pulitzer.

He rises from the table.

Spalding Gray never got a Pulitzer.

He walks into the darkness. From the darkness:

The third day . . .

Light.

. . . after Howard met Don at the motel on the highway, Howard went back to the bench on the beach at the ocean. The day was sunless and dull. It had been dull for weeks. Would the sun ever come out again?

Howard thought about Don.

He wondered if it wasn't too late.

Though dull it had been a warm winter but not nearly warm enough for what Howard was about to do.

He slipped off his shoes and his pants and his shirt and his jacket and folded them neatly and hid them under a fern near the bench. Clearly he had every intention of returning for them; clearly he was just going for a swim.

And so in his boxer shorts and black socks he waded out into the bay without even noticing the blue cold on his skin.

Just past the waist he let go and floated.

Howard loved the water. That's why he didn't want to die by drowning. It wasn't the fish at all. He just didn't want to ruin something wonderful.

But here, floating in the frigid bay, his body numb and calm, he realized just how easy it would be.

Howard put his face in the water, his head under. He held his breath until he almost couldn't anymore.

So easy it would be to just open up now, take it in, take in all the ocean.

To be done.

But then Howard thought about Don. It would be unfair, Howard thought, to break the contract.

Also, he'd already paid. Ten thousand dollars.

Howard was panting as he dragged himself up out of the water onto the shore, and as he lay on the beach, for the first time in weeks, he felt the sun on his body.

And he thinks about BELOVED.

On his way back to the table DANIEL *dashes to the mic.*

Light shift.

HELENA BONHAM CARTER
Hello. Helena Bonham Carter again. Sorry to interrupt but I feel the need to interject because I'm not entirely pleased with my earlier performance as BELOVED. I find the accent tricky. I promise it will improve.

And also I want you to understand I am aware of the implication that Tim's film was connected in some dark way to Spalding Gray's demise. *Big Fish* was the last film Spalding Gray saw, and that night, that last night, he took the ride back and forth, back and forth on the Staten Island Ferry. Trying to decide. To screw up his courage. And it is said that after the movie was over Spalding Gray sat in the theatre and he wept.

So as a result of the film something rose up in him, was ignited, was confirmed perhaps. But in others this rising up, this ignition, this confirmation might lead to a revival of life. And knowing Tim as I do, I am certain this was his intention. So in the case of Spalding, I think it is clear, whatever was broken was already there. But I will admit, at the time, when I heard, I did wonder . . . did we kill Spalding Gray?

At the end of *Big Fish* we come to understand that a person may tell their stories over and over again and in doing so they will become their stories. And because those stories live on after the teller, the storyteller, in effect, becomes immortal.

In the final images of the film the son delivers his dying father to the water and then the father transforms into a big blue fish which leaps up out of the water in a perfect arc and swims away, swims away, swims away.

And I wonder what Spalding Gray was thinking, sitting in a theatre after a film about a father and a son and looking at his own son? How could he still feel so alone? And what was he thinking?

DANIEL goes to the table.

DANIEL
And I wonder what Spalding Gray was thinking, sitting in a theatre after a film about a father and a son and looking at his own son? How could he still feel so alone? And what was he thinking?

He holds up The Journals of Spalding Gray *so that it covers his face.*

SPALDING GRAY
Who cares?

He puts the book down on the table and rests his tired head on the table until:

BELOVED
I care.

I care.

HOWARD
Who are you?

BELOVED
I care.

HOWARD
Who are you?

BELOVED
I'm BELOVED.

HOWARD
No you're not.

BELOVED
Yes I am.

HOWARD
Where did you come from?

BELOVED
I saw you in the market. You laughed. I smiled at you.

HOWARD
Before that. Where did you come from?

BELOVED
From the ocean. From the sky. From swimming.

HOWARD
And one more?

BELOVED
And one more.

HOWARD
From death?

BELOVED
Of course.

HOWARD
Of course.

BELOVED
And I came to tell you something.

HOWARD
What?

BELOVED
It's not your fault.

HOWARD
What?

BELOVED
It's not your fault.

HOWARD
What's not my fault?

BELOVED
It's not your fault how alone you've felt.

It's not your fault you want to be loved.

It's not your fault there was no wind.

She looks at the empty chair.

It's not your fault your mother in the garage.

It's not your fault.

It's not your fault.

She speaks to the audience and slowly becomes DANIEL.

It's not your fault.

It's not your fault.

It's not.

It's not your fault.

It's not your fault.

DANIEL
It's not your fault.

It's not.

It's not your fault.

It's not your fault.

> *DANIEL repeats this until everyone in the audience who needs to be freed of fault is freed of fault.*

And then BELOVED turns into a big blue fish and floats up into the sky and swims away.

> *Light shift.*

And now it's the dream. And I'm in the dream. And you're there. We're all there. And we look like this. And there's a mountain and a Ferris wheel and if you look this way it's all water. Like the ocean. But moreso. And warmer. And it's above us as well. And we're all floating in it. But we don't know. We know but we don't know. The part of us that knows that's the part that wants to swim, and the part of us that doesn't know that's the heavy part. The part that sinks.

> *DANIEL looks at the empty chair.*

The part that doesn't know it can swim.

Slide: "Death."

Light shift.

It's January 12, 2004. San Rafael, California. And I walk into the office of Paul Goodberg, Psychic Surgeon. He asks me how was my night. I tell him I'm feeling a little rough because I went on a pretty serious bender. He says, "Of course. Well that's to be expected." Of course! Why wasn't this guy my therapist all those years? That's to be expected! Thank you.

And I lie on the couch for about an hour. And Paul Goodberg comes out of his trance and tells me: "It is dead."

And as I'm getting ready to leave he tells me that I'm not going to feel myself for a while. I ask him how long. He says, "Three or four years." Yeah well, I haven't felt myself for thirty, what's three or four more. Then I realize I never asked how much this would cost. What with the entity and the danger and everything money didn't seem that significant. So I ask him how much I owe him and he says, "Ten thousand dollars." I blanch. He laughs. The Psychic Surgeon has a sense of humour! And maybe it's his thing, he tells you ten thousand and then when he tells you it's only fifteen hundred you feel like he's giving it away. But even still. This guy killed an entity. If I'd had the ten thousand I probably would have given it to him.

So I write the cheque for fifteen hundred and I leave the office and I am very invested in feeling different but I can't really tell how I feel because I have a wicked hangover. But maybe I feel a little lighter. I walk into the B & B and start packing. I turn on the TV. CNN comes on. Which is not a strange thing. That's how TVs used to work. It comes on the channel you were last watching. And it's been an insane weekend. The entity, the trances, the slaying of the entity, the bender, and I didn't even mention the guy I picked up at the bar because he had coke and brought him back to the B & B. That's another story too long no time can't tell it. It's been a massive three days. But when I turn on the TV and CNN comes on, it's not the weather forecast or a commercial, it's a reporter saying that Spalding Gray is presumed dead. And in that a moment I am certain that I killed Spalding Gray. Did I believe that the next day? Do I believe that now? It doesn't matter, because in that moment I knew I killed Spalding Gray.

DANIEL steps to the mic.

A slide show of the Staten Island Ferry from a rider's POV covers the back wall as he speaks.

He takes a flyer from his back pocket.

The following is read as a eulogy:

"The Staten Island Ferry provides twenty million people a year with ferry service between St. George on Staten Island and Whitehall Street in lower Manhattan. The ferry is the only non-vehicular mode of transportation between Staten Island and Manhattan. Service is provided twenty-four hours a day, 365 days a year. The five-mile journey takes about twenty-five minutes each way. The ferry is free of charge, though for a round trip riders must disembark at each terminal and re-enter through the terminal building to comply with Coast Guard regulations regarding vessel capacity. The Staten Island Ferry is run by the City of New York for one pragmatic reason: to transport Staten Islanders to and from Manhattan. Yet, the five mile, twenty-five minute ride also provides a majestic view of New York Harbour and a no-hassle, even romantic boat ride! One guide book calls it 'One of the world's greatest (and shortest) water voyages.' From the deck of the ferry you will have a perfect view of the Statue of Liberty and Ellis Island. You'll see the skyscrapers and bridges of Lower Manhattan receding as you pull away and coming into focus again as you return.

And it's a free ride."

He returns to the table and sits.

For much of his life Spalding Gray kept journals. Near the end of his life he stopped writing his journal but instead would record his entries. This excerpt was recorded and transcribed. It is dated three weeks before he died.

"And I just can't face . . . dying. Forever and ever and ever and ever and ever and ever and ever and ever and ever and ever and death. Forever and ever and ever and ever and ever and ever and ever and ever and ever and ever and ever and ever. Forever and ever and ever and ever and everevereverevereverever. Oh help me help me help me help me help me help me help me help me help me help me there's nothing to be done, there's nothing to be done, there's nothing to be done."

Light shift.

He rises from the table.

On the fourth day after Howard met Don at the motel on the highway Howard wakes up. He has his coffee, maybe too bitter maybe too weak, it doesn't matter, but it's coffee as always. And he looks at the newspaper as he always does. First at the front section and then the sports and then the arts and the TV listings in case something of interest might be on tonight, in case he comes home alive. And then last, something he started doing only recently, he looks at the obituaries. And there on the page, in black and white, is the name with a picture above. He sees the face first. And then the name "Don Horchuk." Died of a massive coronary at home alone four days ago.

57

That afternoon Howard goes back to the market with the fruits and the nuts and the strange smells. He's half hoping he'll see BELOVED but he knows that's not possible because she turned into a big blue fish and floated away.

He finds himself standing in front of a fruit stall. He sees a fruit he's never seen before. He picks it up. It's hard and brown on the outside, and he imagines that inside it's white and juicy and ripe. He imagines that inside is the rest of his life.

Go.

We hear "This Must Be The Place" by the Talking Heads.

He does a silly dance.

He stops, breathless.

He takes a sip from the glass of water.

He listens as we hear:

ELLAE

So what I feel he's saying now is your expression of him has released him the way somebody who's deeply grieved is released. Grief empowers the thrust of the journey—the more deeply loved a person is the more they're grieved. Now you may feel, you may feel him leaving, you may feel that he's gone. It'll be a good transition and you'll know it when it happens. Have you ever been with someone when they died? There is that feeling when they die that now they're here and now they're gone, and what they left is what they contributed, and it is beautiful. It's a beautiful moment. It's a hallowed moment is what he's saying. It's a hallowed moment and one that he looks forward to experiencing.

He picks up the glass of water.

He stands on the chair.

He raises the glass in a toast.

He pours the water over his head and swims into the sky.

End.

Acknowledgements

Ellae Elinwood, songcarrier@gmail.com
Paul Goodberg, www.helpinghealtheearth.org
Jean and Jeremy Riley
Sherrie Johnson
Gary Markle
Magnetic North Theatre Festival
Luminato
High Performance Rodeo and One Yellow Rabbit
National Arts Centre: Ontario Scene
Judy Laceby and Jane Chalmers
Guntar Kravis
Vince and Frank and Matthew and Alain and Tim and Vincent
and Allan and Darcy and Chris and Peter and Scott and David
and Ryan and Andrew and Daniel and Dave and Gavin and
Jason and Chris and Mathieu and Steven and Joel and Derek
and Joe and Tom and Reid and Bob and Jay and each of their
beloveds

Daniel MacIvor has written many plays, including *See Bob Run*, *Never Swim Alone*, *In On It*, *A Beautiful View*, *His Greatness* and with Daniel Brooks created a series of solo shows that have toured extensively internationally. Daniel received the Governor General's Literary Award for Drama for his collection of plays *I Still Love You* and he was awarded the prestigious Siminovitch Prize in 2008. He is also the recipient of an Obie Award and a GLAAD Award. He is currently based in Halifax, and is developing a new play for Tarragon Theatre called *New Magic Valley Fun Town* and working on the libretto for Rufus Wainwright's *Hadrian*, commissioned by the Canadian Opera Company.

First edition: November 2017

Printed and bound in Canada by Rapido Books, Montreal

The excerpt on page 57 is from *The Journals of Spalding Gray*,
edited by Nell Casey and published by Knopf Doubleday in 2012.

Cover and author photos by Guntar Kravis

PLAYWRIGHTS
CANADA PRESS

202-269 Richmond St. W.

Toronto, ON

M5V 1X1

416.703.0013

info@playwrightscanada.com

www.playwrightscanada.com

@playcanpress